POP PIANO HITS

SIMPLE ARRANGEMENTS FOR STUDENTS OF ALL AGES

Sunflower, Without Me & More Hot Singles

ISBN 978-1-5400-4937-7

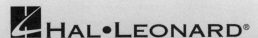

Visit Hal Leonard Online at
www.halleonard.com

Contact us:
Hal Leonard
7777 West Bluemound Road
Milwaukee, WI 53213
Email: info@halleonard.com

In Europe, contact:
Hal Leonard Europe Limited
42 Wigmore Street
Marylebone, London, W1U 2RN
Email: info@halleonardeurope.com

In Australia, contact:
Hal Leonard Australia Pty. Ltd.
4 Lentara Court
Cheltenham, Victoria, 3192 Australia
Email: info@halleonard.com.au

Contents

HIGH HOPES

Words and Music by BRENDON URIE, SAMUEL HOLLANDER,
WILLIAM LOBBAN BEAN, JONAS JEBERG,
JACOB SINCLAIR, JENNY OWEN YOUNGS,
ILSEY JUBER, LAUREN PRITCHARD
and TAYLOR PARKS

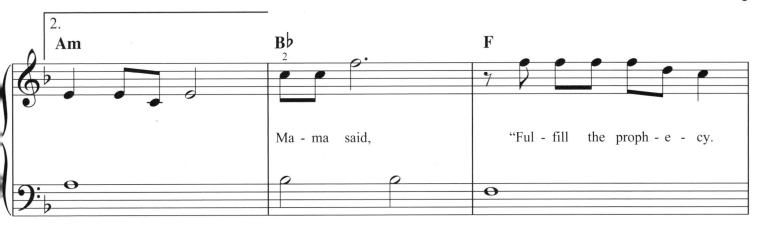

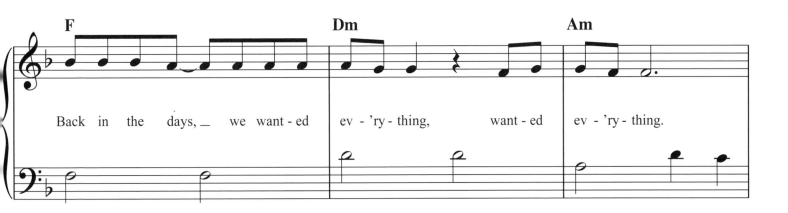

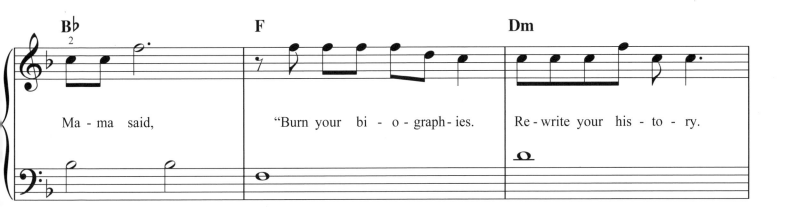

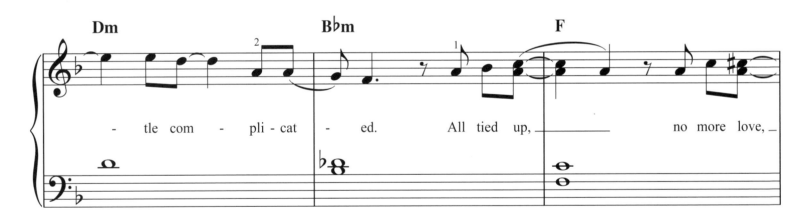

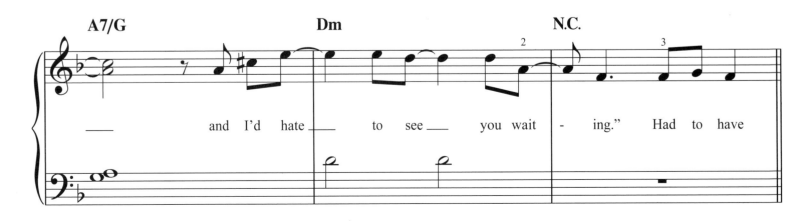

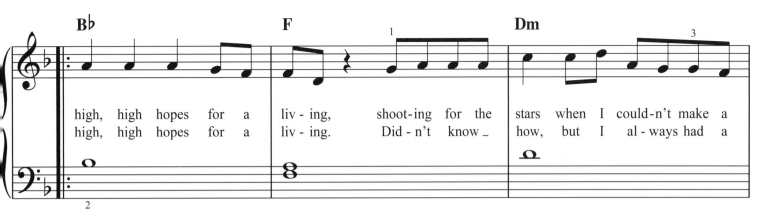

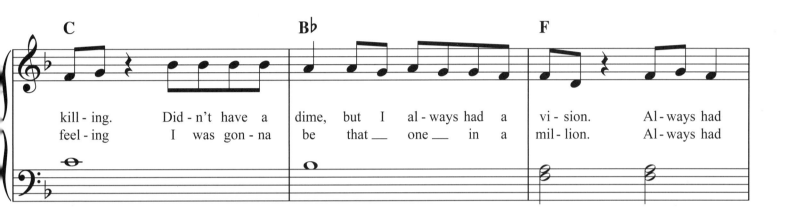

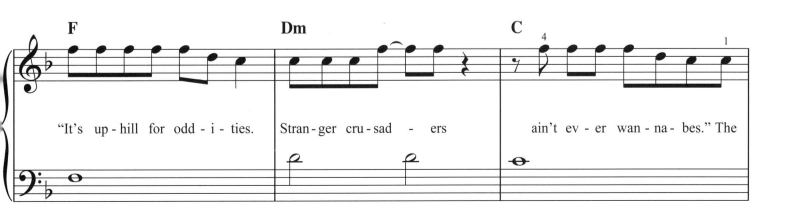

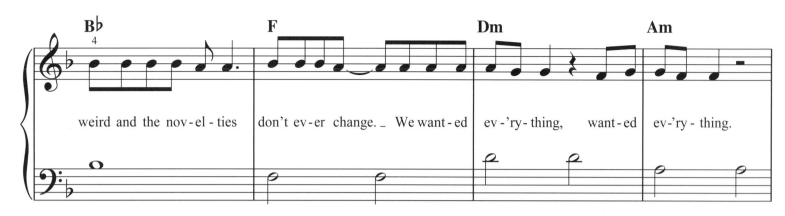

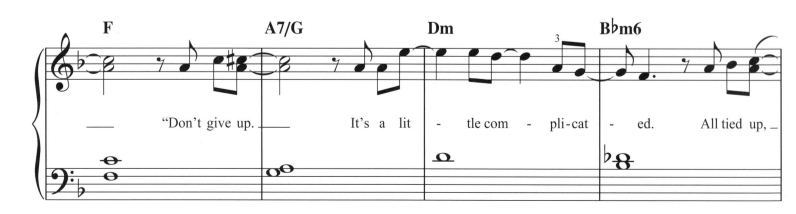

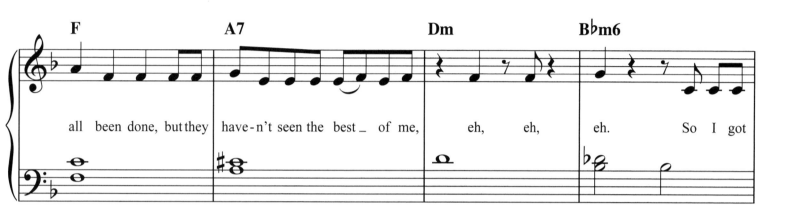

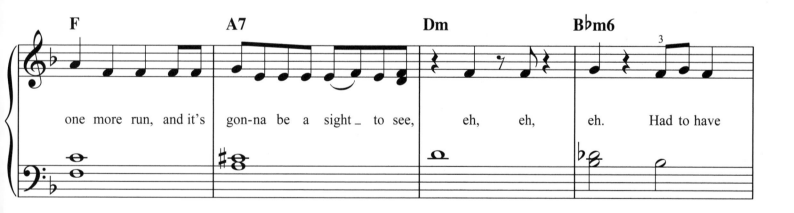

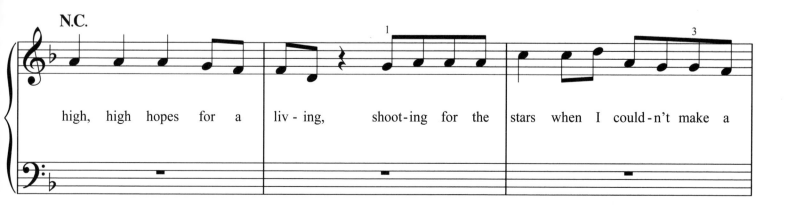

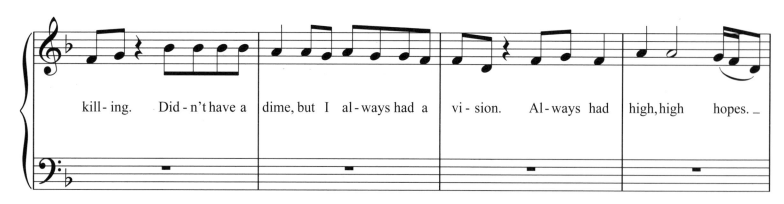

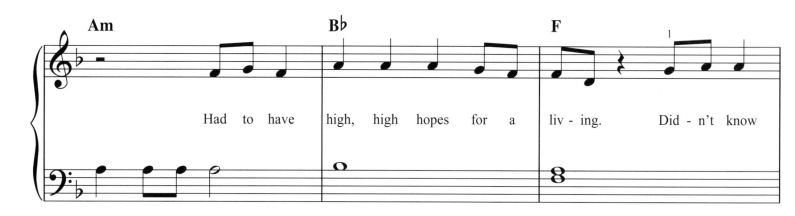

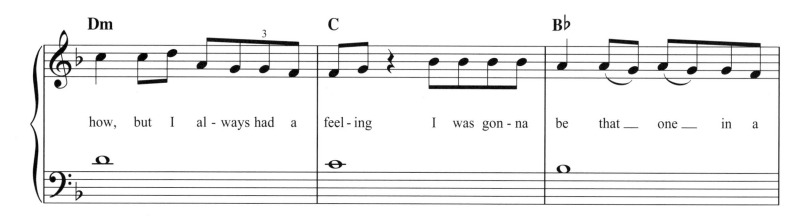

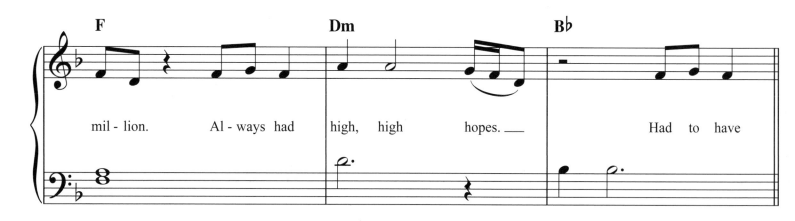

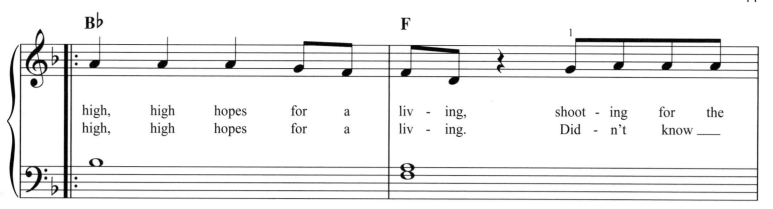

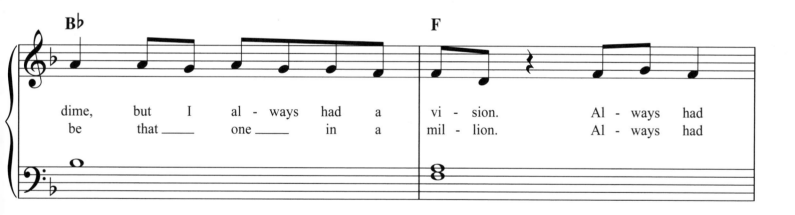

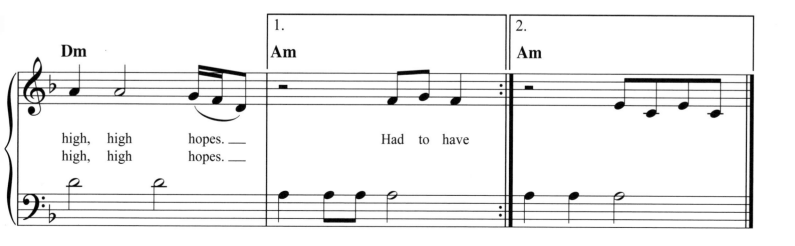

SHALLOW

from A STAR IS BORN

Words and Music by STEFANI GERMANOTTA,
MARK RONSON, ANDREW WYATT
and ANTHONY ROSSOMANDO

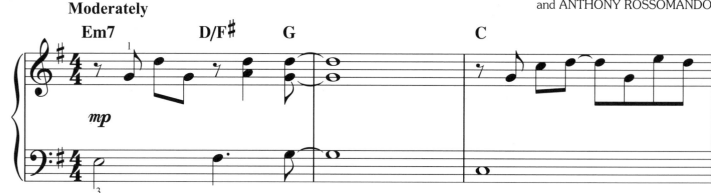

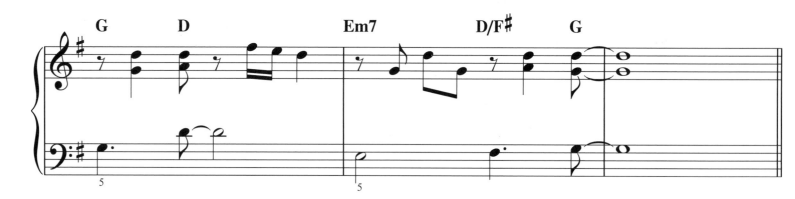

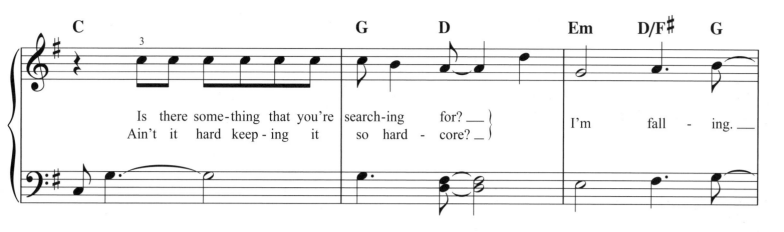

Is there some-thing that you're searching for? ___
Ain't it hard keep-ing it so hard-core? ___

I'm fall - ing. ___

___ In all the good times I find my-self ___ long-ing ___

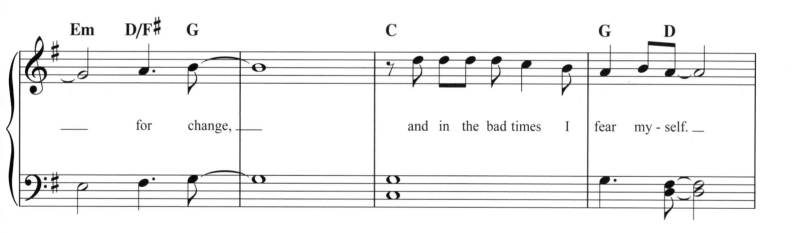

___ for change, ___ and in the bad times I fear my-self. ___

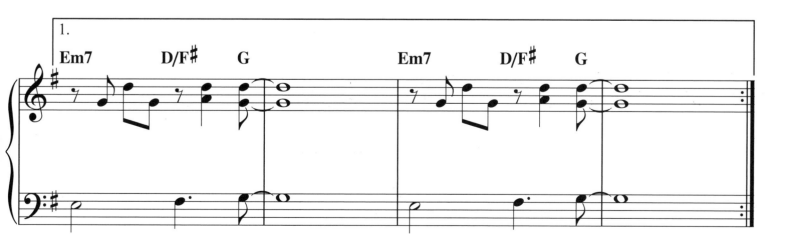

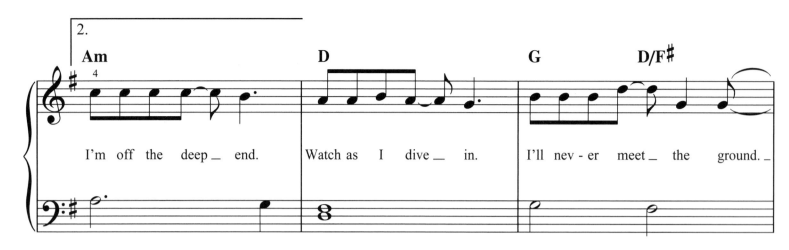

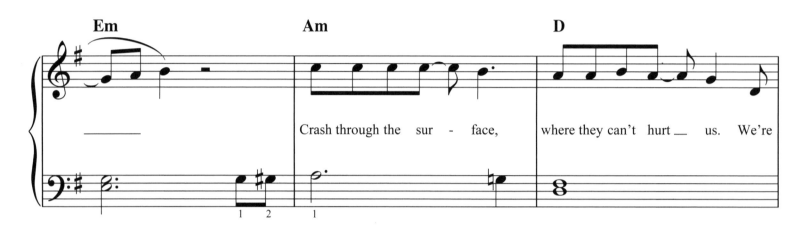

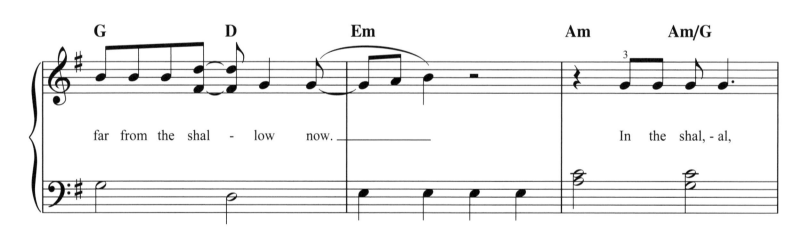

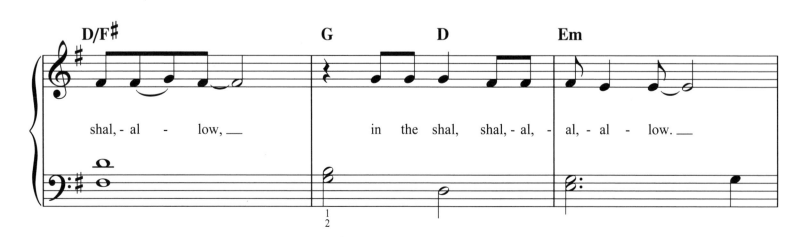

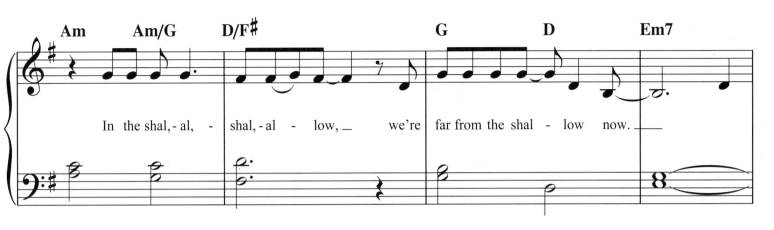

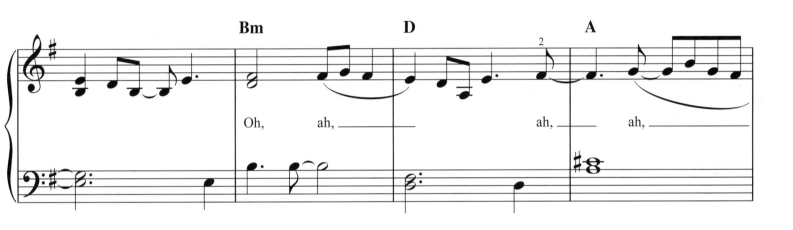

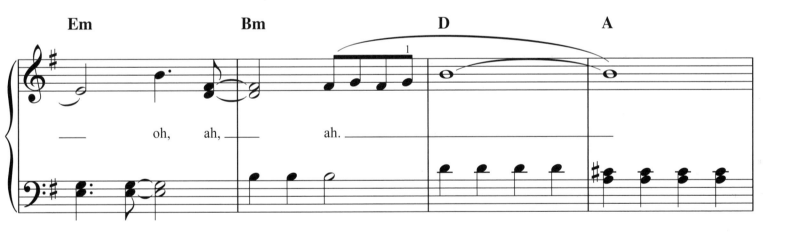

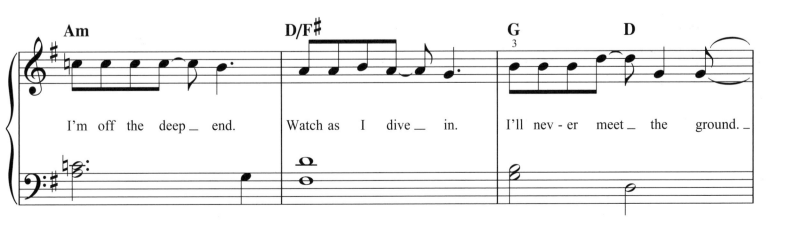

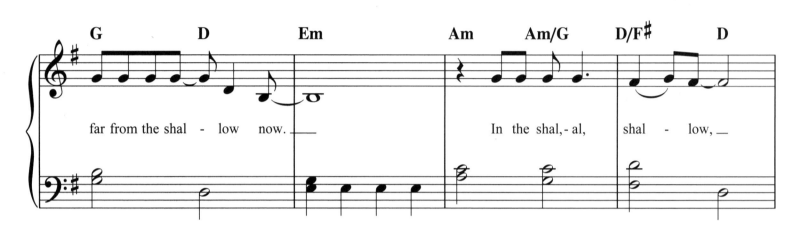

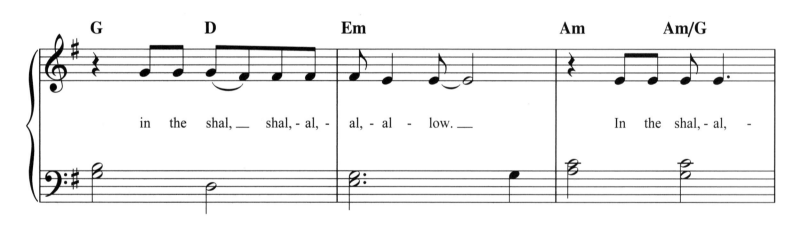

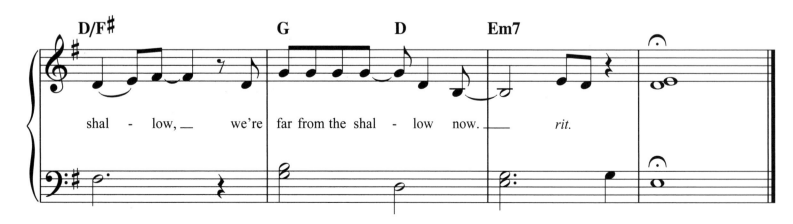

NO PLACE LIKE YOU

Words and Music by TROY VERGES,
BRETT JAMES and JOSHUA MILLER

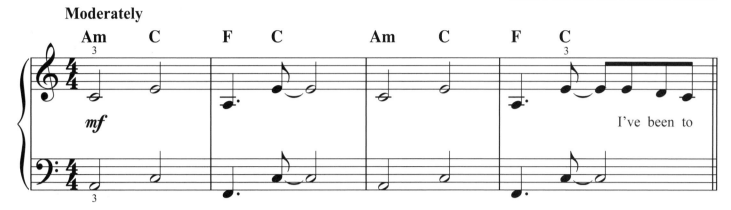

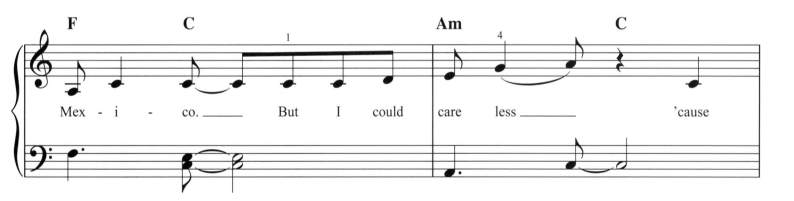

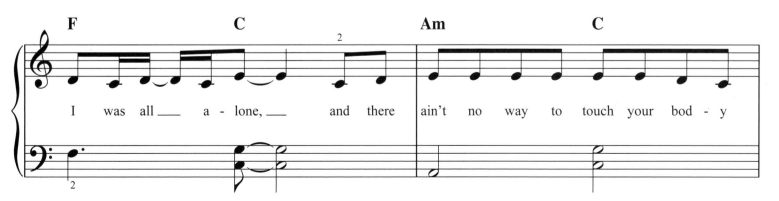

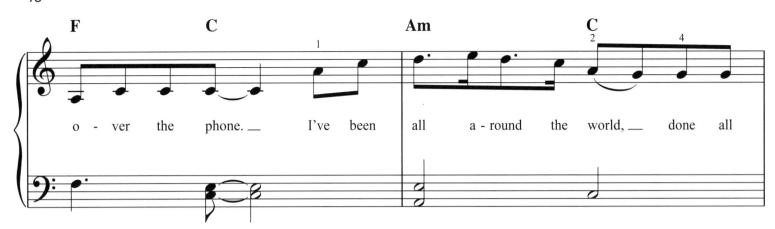

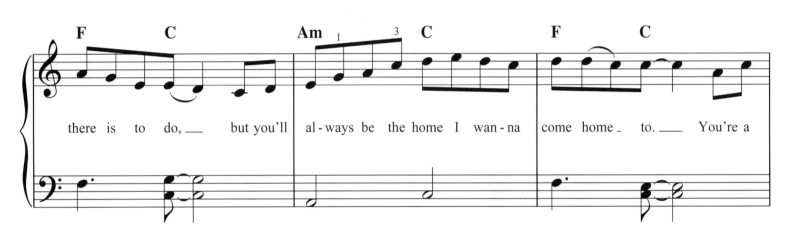

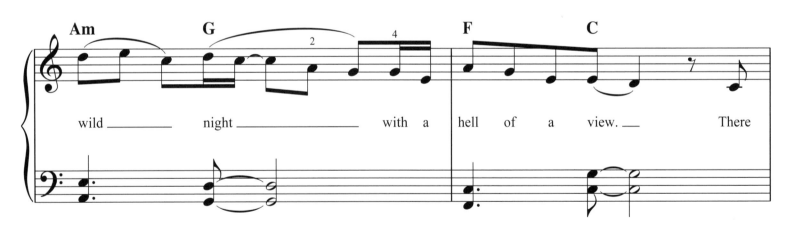

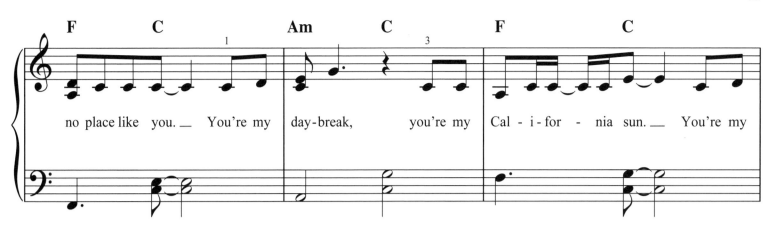

no place like you. __ You're my day-break, you're my Cal - i - for - nia sun. __ You're my

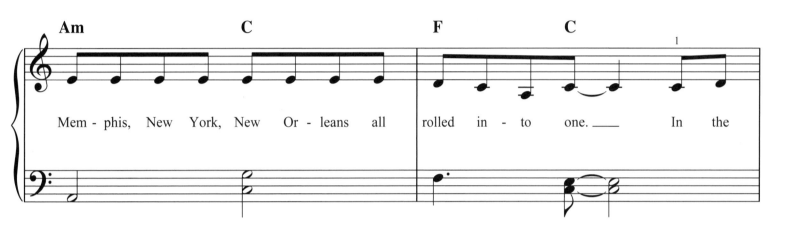

Mem - phis, New York, New Or - leans all rolled in - to one. ____ In the

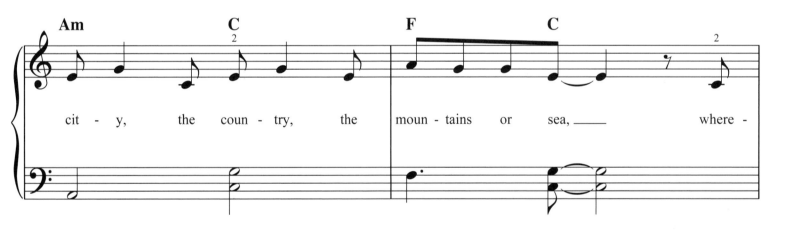

cit - y, the coun - try, the moun - tains or sea, ____ where -

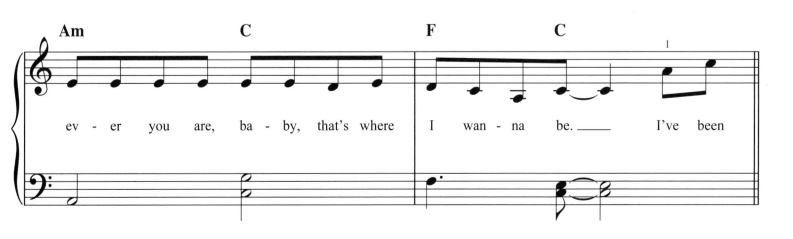

ev - er you are, ba - by, that's where I wan - na be. ____ I've been

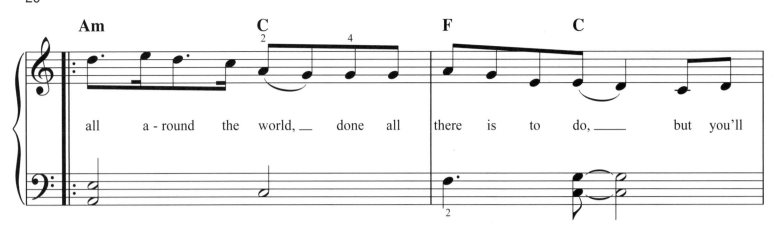

all a-round the world, __ done all there is to do, ____ but you'll

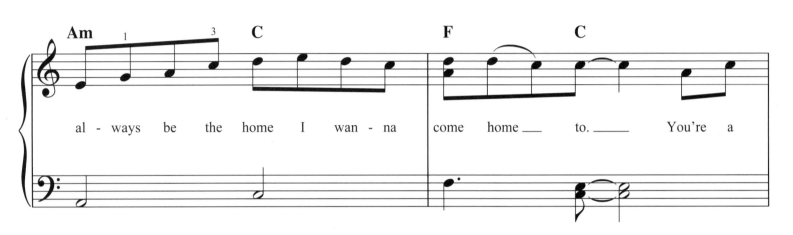

al-ways be the home I wan-na come home __ to. ____ You're a

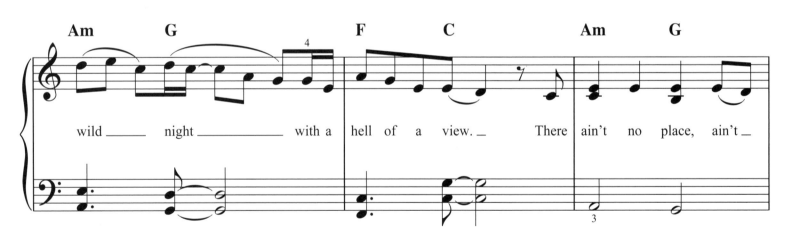

wild ____ night _____ with a hell of a view. __ There ain't no place, ain't __

no place like you. __ There ain't no place, ain't __ no place like you. __

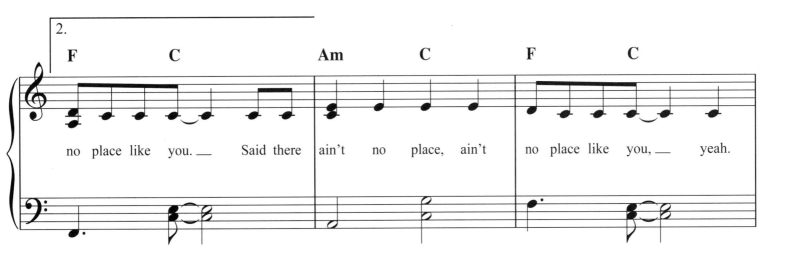

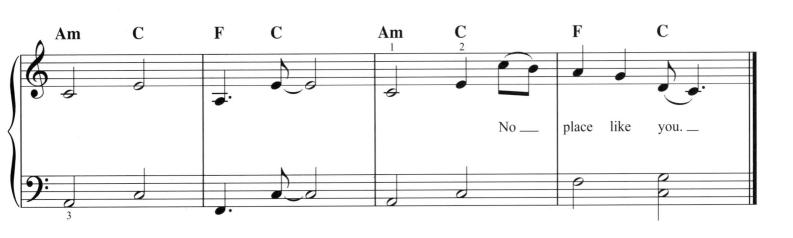

SUNFLOWER
from SPIDER-MAN: INTO THE SPIDER-VERSE

Words and Music by AUSTIN RICHARD POST,
LOUIS BELL, SWAE LEE, BILLY WALSH,
CARL ROSEN, CARTER LANG
and KHALIF BROWN

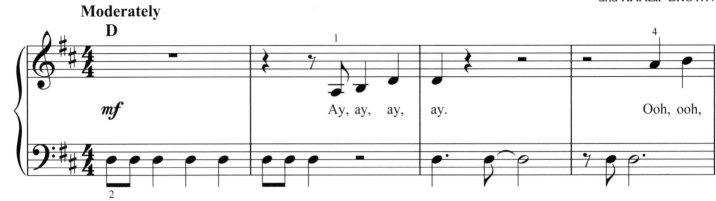

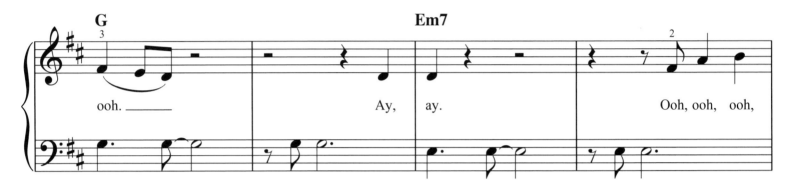

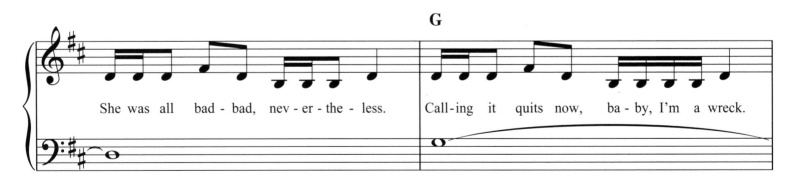

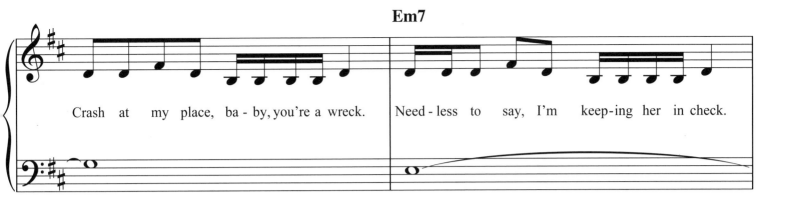

Em7

Crash at my place, ba - by, you're a wreck. Need - less to say, I'm keep-ing her in check.

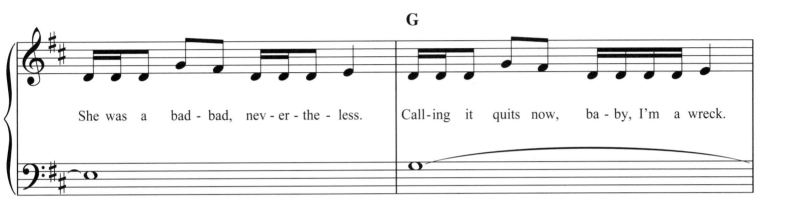

G

She was a bad - bad, nev - er - the - less. Call-ing it quits now, ba - by, I'm a wreck.

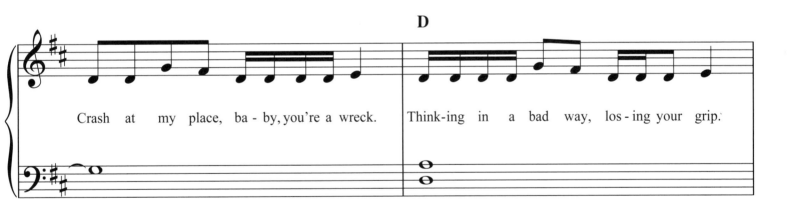

D

Crash at my place, ba - by, you're a wreck. Think-ing in a bad way, los - ing your grip.

G

Scream-ing at my face, ba - by, don't trip. Some-one took a big L, don't know how that felt. __

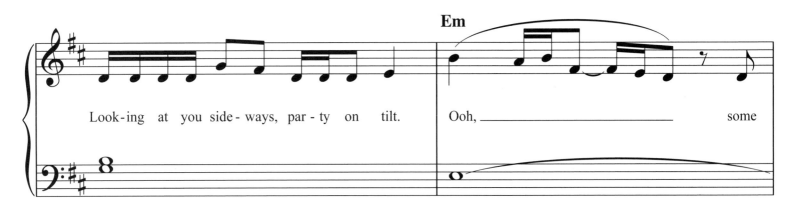

Look-ing at you side-ways, par-ty on tilt. Ooh, _____ some

things you just can't re-fuse. _____ She wan-na ride like a cruise, _____ and I'm

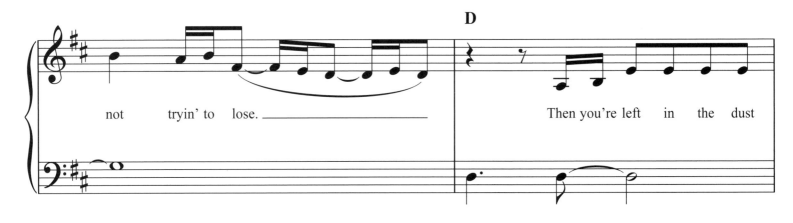

not tryin' to lose. _____ Then you're left in the dust

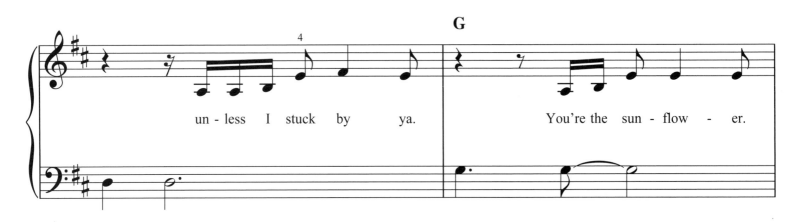

un-less I stuck by ya. You're the sun-flow-er.

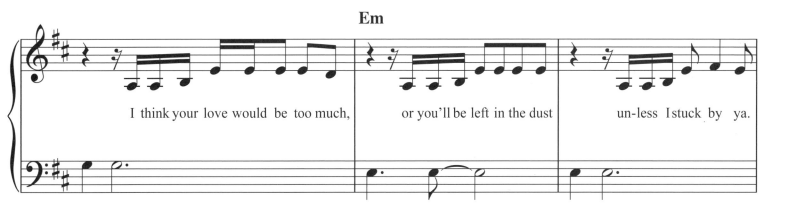

I think your love would be too much,   or you'll be left in the dust   un-less I stuck by ya.

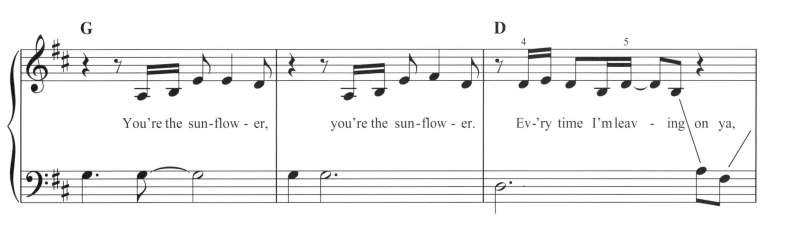

You're the sun-flow - er,   you're the sun-flow - er.   Ev-'ry time I'm leav - ing on ya,

you don't make it eas - y, no.   Wish I could be ___ there for ya.

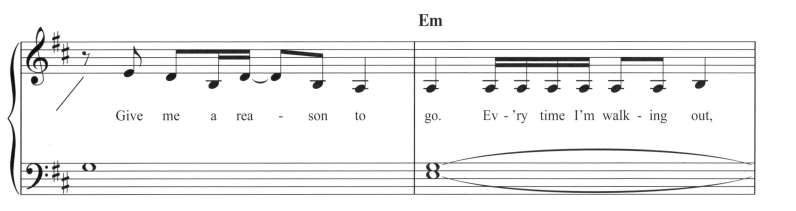

Give me a rea - son to   go.   Ev-'ry time I'm walk - ing out,

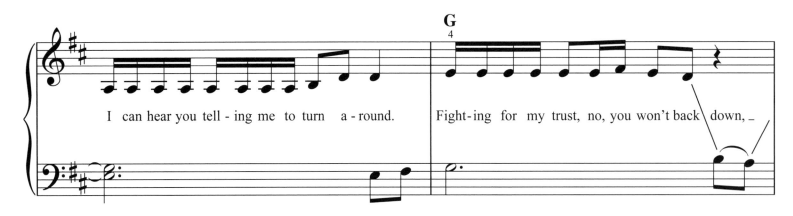

I can hear you tell-ing me to turn a-round. Fight-ing for my trust, no, you won't back down, __

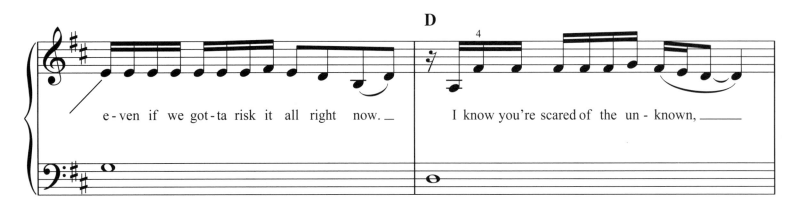

e-ven if we got-ta risk it all right now. __ I know you're scared of the un-known, _____

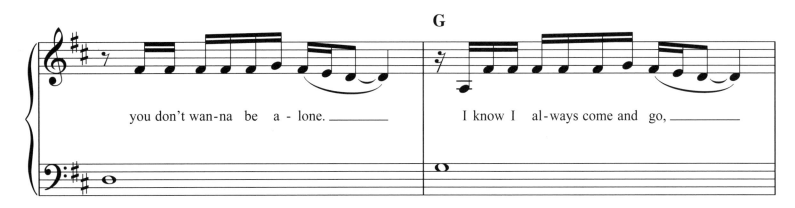

you don't wan-na be a-lone. _____ I know I al-ways come and go, _____

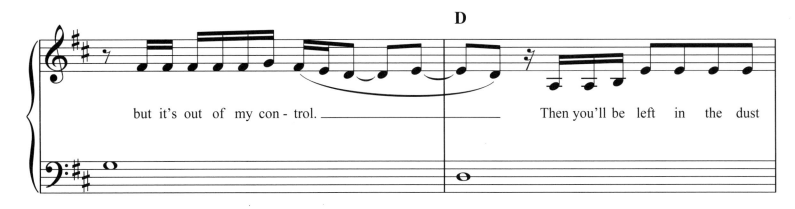

but it's out of my con-trol. _____ Then you'll be left in the dust

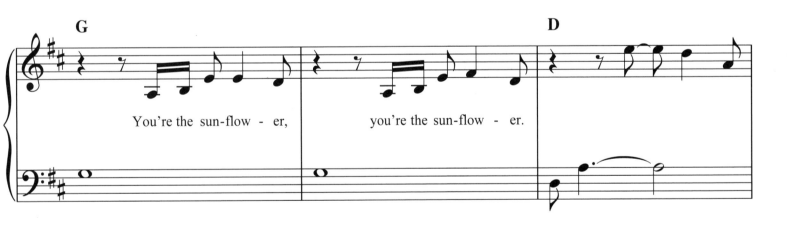

WITHOUT ME

Words and Music by ASHLEY FRANGIPANE,
BRITTANY AMARADIO, CARL ROSEN,
JUSTIN TIMBERLAKE, SCOTT STORCH,
LOUIS BELL, AMY ALLEN
and TIMOTHY MOSLEY

Slow R&B groove

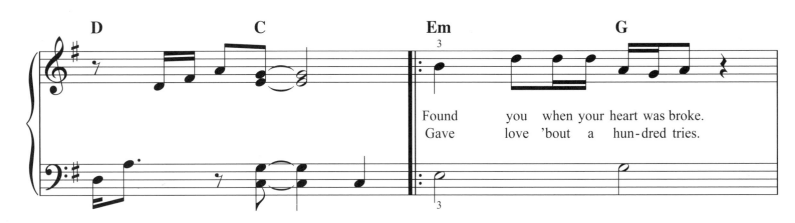

Found you when your heart was broke.
Gave love 'bout a hun-dred tries.

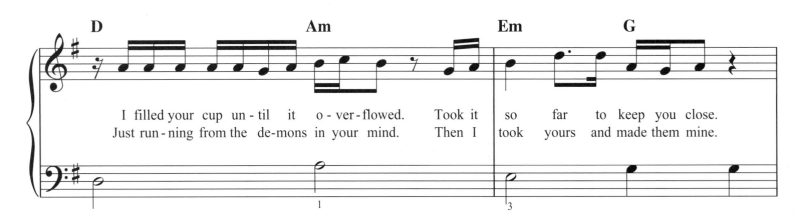

I filled your cup un-til it o-ver-flowed. Took it so far to keep you close.
Just run-ning from the de-mons in your mind. Then I took yours and made them mine.

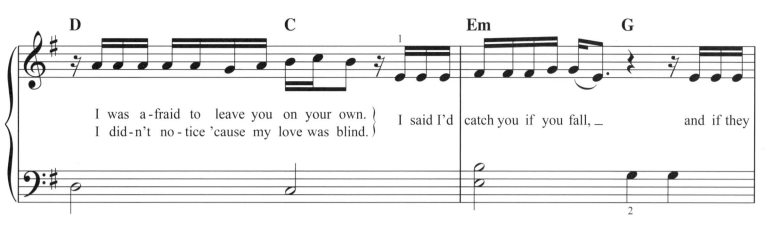

I was a-fraid to leave you on your own.
I did-n't no-tice 'cause my love was blind.
I said I'd catch you if you fall, __ and if they

laugh, then leave 'em all. __ And then I got you off your knees, put you right back on your feet just so

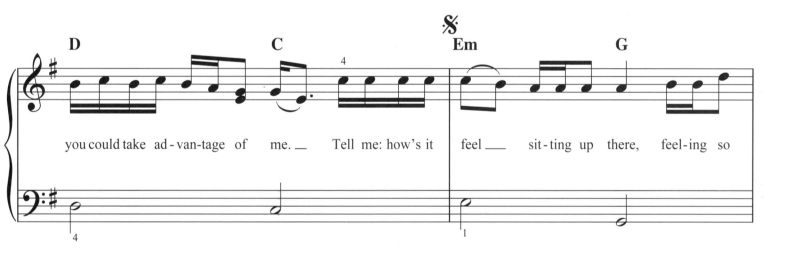

you could take ad-van-tage of me. __ Tell me: how's it feel __ sit-ting up there, feel-ing so

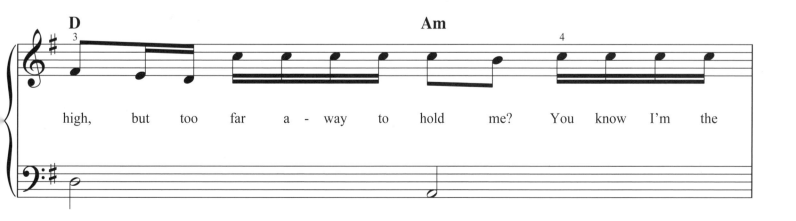

high, but too far a-way to hold me? You know I'm the

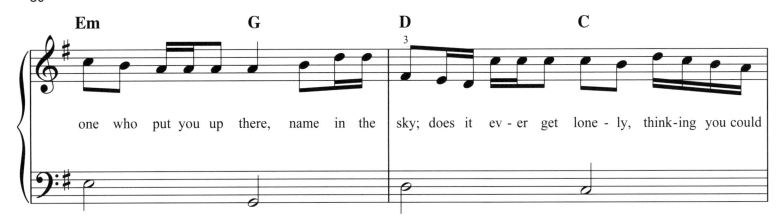

one who put you up there, name in the sky; does it ev-er get lone-ly, think-ing you could

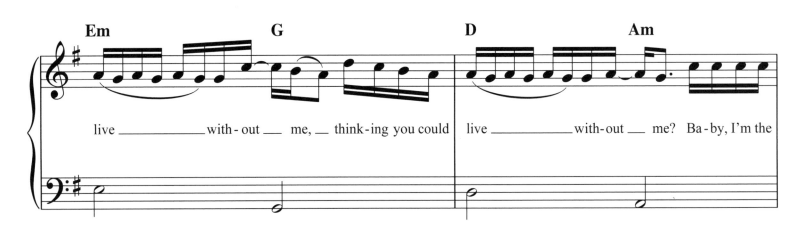

live _____ with-out ___ me, ___ think-ing you could live _____ with-out ___ me? Ba-by, I'm the

To Coda

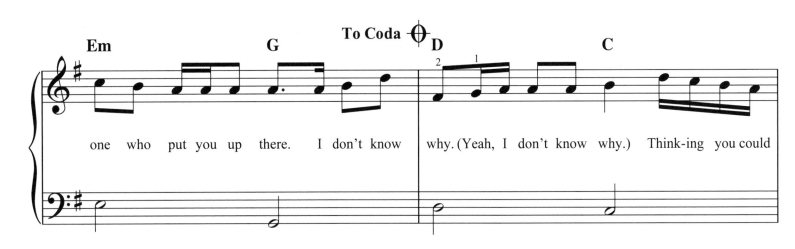

one who put you up there. I don't know why. (Yeah, I don't know why.) Think-ing you could

live _____ with-out ___ me, ___ live _____ with-out ___ me? Ba-by, I'm the

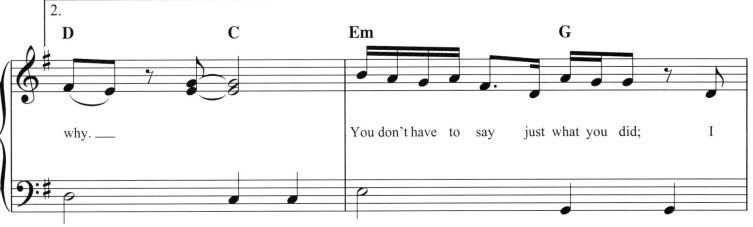

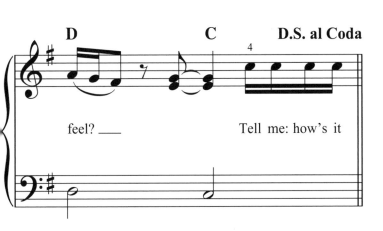

POP PIANO HITS

Pop Piano Hits is a series designed for students of all ages. Each book contains five simple and easy-to-read arrangements of today's most popular downloads. Lyrics, fingering and chord symbols are included to help you make the most of each arrangement. Enjoy your favorite songs and artists today!

BELIEVER, WHAT ABOUT US & MORE HOT SINGLES

Attention (Charlie Puth) • Believer (Imagine Dragons) • There's Nothing Holdin' Me Back (Shawn Mendes) • Too Good at Goodbyes (Sam Smith) • What About Us (P!nk).
00251934 Easy Piano................\$9.99

BLANK SPACE, I REALLY LIKE YOU & MORE HOT SINGLES

Blank Space (Taylor Swift) • Heartbeat Song (Kelly Clarkson) • I Really Like You (Carly Rae Jepsen) • I'm Not the Only One (Sam Smith) • Thinking Out Loud (Ed Sheeran).
00146286 Easy Piano................\$9.99

CAN'T STOP THE FEELING, 7 YEARS & MORE HOT SINGLES

Can't Stop the Feeling (Justin Timberlake) • H.O.L.Y. (Florida Georgia Line) • Just Like Fire (Pink) • Lost Boy (Ruth B.) • 7 Years (Lukas Graham).
00193755 Easy Piano................\$9.99

CITY OF STARS, MERCY & MORE HOT SINGLES

City of Stars (from *La La Land*) • Evermore (from Beauty and the Beast) • Mercy (Shawn Mendes) • Perfect (Ed Sheeran) • Stay (Zedd & Alessia Cara).
00236097 Easy Piano................\$9.99

FEEL IT STILL, REWRITE THE STARS & MORE HOT SINGLES

Feel It Still (Portugal. The Man) • Lost in Japan (Shawn Mendes) • The Middle (Zedd, Maren Morris & Grey) • Rewrite the Stars (from *The Greatest Showman*) • Whatever It Takes (Imagine Dragons).
00278090 Easy Piano................\$9.99

GIRLS LIKE YOU, HAPPY NOW & MORE HOT SINGLES

Girls Like You (Maroon 5) • Happy Now (Zedd feat. Elley Duhé) • Treat Myself (Meghan Trainor) • You Are the Reason (Calum Scott) • You Say (Lauren Daigle).
00285014 Easy Piano................\$9.99

HOW FAR I'LL GO, THIS TOWN & MORE HOT SINGLES

How Far I'll Go (Alessia Cara - from *Moana*) • My Way (Calvin Harris) • This Town (Niall Horan) • Treat You Better (Shawn Mendes) • We Don't Talk Anymore (Charlie Puth feat. Selena Gomez).
00211286 Easy Piano................\$9.99

LET IT GO, HAPPY & MORE HOT SINGLES

All of Me (John Legend) • Dark Horse (Katy Perry) • Happy (Pharrell) • Let It Go (Demi Lovato) • Pompeii (Bastille).
00128204 Easy Piano................\$9.99

LOVE YOURSELF, STITCHES & MORE HOT SINGLES

Like I'm Gonna Lose You (Meghan Trainor) • Love Yourself (Justin Bieber) • One Call Away (Charlie Puth) • Stitches (Shawn Mendes) • Stressed Out (Twenty One Pilots).
00159285 Easy Piano................\$9.99

ROAR, ROYALS & MORE HOT SINGLES

Atlas (Coldplay – from *The Hunger Games: Catching Fire*) • Roar (Katy Perry) • Royals (Lorde) • Safe and Sound (Capital Cities) • Wake Me Up! (Avicii).
00123868 Easy Piano................\$9.99

SAY SOMETHING, COUNTING STARS & MORE HOT SINGLES

Counting Stars (One Republic) • Demons (Imagine Dragons) • Let Her Go (Passenger) • Say Something (A Great Big World) • Story of My Life (One Direction).
00125356 Easy Piano................\$9.99

SEE YOU AGAIN, FLASHLIGHT & MORE HOT SINGLES

Budapest (George Ezra) • Flashlight (Jessie J.) • Honey I'm Good (Andy Grammer) • See You Again (Wiz Khalifa) • Shut Up and Dance (Walk the Moon).
00150045 Easy Piano................\$9.99

SHAKE IT OFF, ALL ABOUT THAT BASS & MORE HOT SINGLES

All About That Bass (Meghan Trainor) • Shake It Off (Taylor Swift) • A Sky Full of Stars (Coldplay) • Something in the Water (Carrie Underwood) • Take Me to Church (Hozier).
00142734 Easy Piano................\$9.99

SUNFLOWER, WITHOUT ME & MORE HOT SINGLES

High Hopes (Panic! at the Disco) • No Place (Backstreet Boys) • Shallow (Lady Gaga and Bradley Cooper) • Sunflower (Post Malone) • Without Me (Halsey).
00291634 Easy Piano................\$9.99

HAL•LEONARD®

www.halleonard.com